MW00624249

Also by Peter O'Leary

THE SAMPO

THE

PETER
O'LEARY

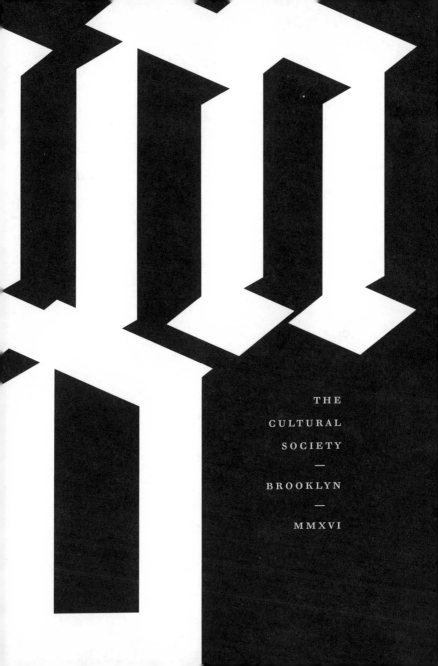

THE
CULTURAL
SOCIETY
—
BROOKLYN
—
MMXVI

for my mother

I. FORGING THE SAMPO

—

TO FORGE. TO FORAGE. TO FORGE. The boreal
forest—

icing on the fronds of pines. Snow lodes caught at
the cores of trees. Hovering

winter sun. Pale. Its approaching mid-day hiatus.
Reindeer. His horse.

Motifs woven on its harness. Rimed. Tinkle of the
bells.

Absorbed by the snowy fields. Hiss of his sledge.
Cutting birchwood runners.

Deerskins. Elks' antlers. Clean cold he rolls
through.

And there: at last. A birch tree.

Stripped of leaves. Mycophoric birch. Branches
witching outward.

This specimen: sorcery's northmost sign. Polished
   wedge of wood rubbed smoother still.
Birch. *Koivu.* In his pocket. Talismanic sympath
   of the southerly
woods. His power. Väinämöinen. Sighing. Talking.
"Wolves devour wizards. Disease fells Fenni.
   Easily as trees.
'You'll never make it!' So they said. Doomed
   journey. Neither
tooth of wolf nor claw of frost assailed me."
   Blessed birch!
Ramifying underground. Shining moonlight! It's
   only afternoon.
Pluming breath. His mirth. His moustaches
   sodden. From breathing
heavily. The wood's cool blue doom.

Moon like a torch fuse. Moon like a redolence of
   life. A force. A smear.
Väinämöinen. Feeling at his feet earthen powers.
   Väinämöinen. An incitation,

a feeling of the turning world. An opening in the
  grove. Spied there. Sudden
kratophanic onset. Sense of instant forces. Issuing
  into him. Singing.

Väinämöinen. Singing spruces.
Into life. And birches crowned in
golden leaves all shining. Birches
lords of evening's shadows brighter

than the moon. Its silver corona. Väinämöinen.
  Summoning trees—
birches, firs—infused with vernal novum.
Songs of magic. Moonlight. In argentine fir tips.
  Ursine starlight.
In the branches. Cool clouds in tatters.

Resinous evergreens. Spruces sung to awesome
  heights.
Väinämöinen. Shaman lord. Wizard singer. His
  courser strong.

Bolting suddenly onward. His speed. Through the
　　forestum. Its incantatory

foreordination. Loosening the hallucinations.

Heaven frost. Skillful spreading. Down into the
　　earth. Tremendous speed

of his horse. Rushing to his home. His mind in
　　gloom. Tilt of his felted cap.

Troublesome task ahead of him. Ilmarinen. The
　　great smith. His one friend.

Whose skills he'd promised to the dark North
　　Country.

In exchange for his own life. Pohjola. Darkest
　　realm. Witch infested.

Poor of light. Dreary Sariola. Darkness
　　homestead.

Then, his horse, halting. At Osmo. At the foot of
　　the coal shed. The workshop glowing. Bright.

Inside, a heaved sound of iron being shaped. A
　　hammer's earthen thud. Outlandish

emanations of heat. Washing over him. From the
    forge. Where Ilmarinen toils.
Carbonite mystery maker. Who says, looking up,
"Väinämöinen! Where've you been?"

"In the North. Padding its snowfields on
    snowshoes.
Learning the boreal sorceries. Foraging the lore
    there with makers
of magic. On the shelves of ice. In the treeless
    wastes. Looking
for the hidden threads. In a gloom. A
    dumbfounding.
Pohjola. Darkest realm. Witch infested. Poor of
    light.
Dreary Sariola. Darkness homestead."

Forge. Hammer. Tongs. Loose lashings of flame.
    From the oven.
Ilmarinen. Wood cords of his forearms. Skunking

musk of his beard. Heat. Smokehouse
of his woolen vest. Rank in its coils of fabric.
Great ursus of his working form. Sensing
    something coming. *What?*

Cunning Väinämöinen. In the hearth light.
    Pacing gently.
His deceptions. Coming. "There's a great beauty
    who takes no suitors.
A virgin. In Pohjola. Dwelling in moonlight.
Radiating sunbeams.
On her shoulders, the Great Bear shining.
On her back, the Seven Stars mapped.
Ilmarinen. My one friend. Go north. Get her.
    Woo her. Forge before her the Sampo. Its
intricate, interlocking lid. Its image of the starry
    sphere.
Its mirror of the underworld channels.
Its forest of root systems. Its agarical
jewels. Go north. Go do it."

And Ilmarinen. Tongs in hand. Clasping coals.
"Devourers of human flesh. Drowners of the
    masters of love.
Dreary Sariola?! That witch-infested darkness
    homestead.
I'm not going. Never."

Then Väinämöinen. Illusionist. Offering instead.
"Come see this. An unreal wonder. A spruce.
    Crowned
in blooming flowers. With endless leaves
of gold. Moon on its crown. In its branches,
the Great Bear resting."

And Ilmarinen. "Not possible. Not in this winter.
    Show me."

Coursers. Through the snowfields. Hammering.
    To outside Osmo. Site
of Väinämöinen's summoning. Wherefrom
he feels the turning of the world.

There. The spruce, ablaze.
In the moonlight.
Amazement.

Then Väinämöinen. "Climb it, smith. Get the
　　moon. Coax down the Great Bear."

And Ilmarinen. Hoisting himself up. Surprising
　　deftness of his climbing.
Flowing up into the tree. Like a bear himself.
　　Like smoke.

Swaying now in the top of the spruce. *Fool*. You
　　child. That's the moon reflected from its
　　needles. And those
are great glisters of ice.
And Väinämöinen. Power streaming upward
　　through him—great rotations
fluming the air around him.
Huge winds. Wild crippled epilepsy.

Of all the trees in sudden motion. Frantic
passing of the winds. From branch to branch.

From tree to tree. Their
furious intensification. "Take the smith, winds.
Carry him. Like a boat. Tossed in stormy waters.
To the glooms."

Moon the winds howl toward. Sun that buffets
     them in
thermal harm. Great Bear's shoulders they rake.
Northland sauna road they track.
Three main rooms of the world they ventilate and
     shape.

And so the smith is taken. Harnessed to those
     furies. Whipped by those
instantaneous terrors. To dreary Sariola. Pohjola.
     Poor
of light. Witch infested. Darkness homestead.

Realm of fields with serpents writhing in them.
Realm of daemonically changing forms: bear and
  wolf.
Realm of huge and terrible pike.
Realm of dogs. Tails suddenly still. Swallowing
  their barks.

Louhi. Gap-toothed hag of Pohjola.
"You. Who are you that watchdogs hold their
  warning barks?"

Ilmarinen. "A stranger.
Wind's captive."

Then Louhi. "Do you know of Ilmarinen—
the smith whose skills we need.
To forge anew.
In the darkness.
A Sampo."

And Ilmarinen. Wood cords of his forearms.
Skunking musk of his beard.
Stain of frigid wind in it. Great
ursus of his working form.
"I'm him."

Louhi. Slipping away inside. To the virgin.
    Coaxing her to come out.
Making her prettier. Emphasizing
her lovely body. With headbands. Copper
    bracelets. Golden hoops. Silver
threaded in her hair.
Her shining
cheeks.

Beauty. Of the North Country. She's outside. And
    suddenly it's summer.

Ilmarinen. Guided by her hand so soft. Simple
    cabins

they live in. Great shapely shadows of the
    interiors.
Hearth of light. Smell of woodsmoke. Saturating
the thatch of the roof, bright red colors
of the woven hangings. Long table. Worn bench
    alongside. Rubbed smooth from use.
Cheeses. Cured meats and smoked pike.
    Unleavened disk of rye—
still warm. Spread with egg butter. And rice
    custard.
She feeds him. Gives him beer.
Implies her desire.

Fuck her. He wants to fuck her.

The maiden, speaking. "The Sampo. Forge it.
    For us."
And Ilmarinen. Not pausing. "I'll forge it. The
    Sampo. Its intricate
interlocking lid. Its image of the starry sphere.

Its mirror of the underworld channels.
I'll hammer it. Form wholly wrought.
But fangled and fine.

These I'll want. A swan's wing tips. Finely
    grooved.
A barren cow's acrid milk.
A grain of barley.
A ewe's newly sheered wool.

Heaven's the first lid I ever forged. The dome of
    sky
I hammered out. From nothing.
There's my skill.

Where's my forge and where's my smithy.
Where's my hammer. Where my tongs. Anvil.
    Mallet. Bellows.
With these I'll forge. In the woodlands.
Forest allies. Guiding me. By scent and aspect."

And with that, setting off.
Into the woods.

Crimson flesh. Fleecy remnants on the caps.
  Pushing through the pine duff.
Leading Ilmarinen. Deeper into the trees.
Lucid-looking amanitas.
Sifts of light. Bright red dottles.
His attention. Expanded.
Sweet wandering. A day. Then days.

There. Huge. A stone. Streaked with color.
  Hematite.
Troop of amanitas. In a circle around it.
Rhizomorphs.
Changing forms.
Profundities. Outside the body.

Colossal wall of stone behind the streaked one.
  Here. The smith. Banking his fire.
For a whole day. Building an oven.

Intense heat. Reflecting off the wall. Dry
agonized branches of fir. Snap
of broken bone. The sound. A roar.
Feeding the blaze.

The next day. Building his forge.
Curious serfs. Assembling to watch a master
    working.
Great ursus of his form. Nimbleness of gesture.
    A movement like dancing.

Ilmarinen. Felled log for a level. To the bellows
    that he built there.
Endless midnight twilight of the midsummer.
Come upon him. Cinders in radiating plumes.
"You there. You seven.
Work the bellows."

Immense unruly heat in the scene. Competing
    solar source

of the fire. Thrust beneath the forge.
By the smith.
His deft
craft.

Three long summer days. The seven serfs.
   Pumping the bellows. Three expansive
summer evenings. Stones.
Glowing beneath their feet. Unremitting labor.
   Epic
time. And Ilmarinen. Forging.

Intense immensus of the fire. Forge as
   self-manifestation.
Searching there. In its flames.

A bow. A boat. A heifer. A plow.
One a day for four days revealed. Grown from
   fire.

Each ill.
Wicked.
Evil.

Bow of gold tipped in silver, with arrow shafts of
    shining copper.
Boat whose prow is colored gold, oarlocks
    wrought from polished copper.
Heifer idol cast in chromy gold. Great
    constellation spangling her forehead.
Golden corona encircling her horns.
Plow of shining gold with handles tipped in silver.

Each object an evil waster of plenty.
Men the bow would slay.
Wars the boat would wage.
Milk of honey the heifer would spill.
Meadows the plow would thrash.

One each day. Each day crushed. Smashed. By
    Ilmarinen

destroyed. Urging the seven serfs
to pump the bellows harder.
To the limit of their powers.

Winds. In great thrashing roars.
The eastern wind first. Unleashed. Then the
    gusting western wind.
Tantrums of the southern winds.
Thermal furies from the ice cap's northern winds.
Three days blowing in succession. All the while
    the great billows
pumping.

Fire flashing on glass.
Cinders pluming up to the forge of heaven.
Smoke of the sky. Fume of flame and wind.

Sign of Ilmarinen's making. Unremitting
    movement of his ursine form.

There. After three days. In the bottom of the
   furnace.
The Sampo. Forming. Like a pyromantic morel.
   In the ashes.
Its many-colored cap. Lustrous and waxy. Fuse of
   force pushing it from flame
into life.

And Ilmarinen. Flexing his fist on the shaft of his
   hammer.
And with his tongs pulling the Sampo. From the
   heart of the fire.
Shaping for the maiden this vivid form.
Its intricate interlocking lid. Its image of the
   starry sphere.
Its mirror of the underworld channels.
Its forest of root systems.
Its agarical jewels.
Welding it.
Hammering it.
Heaping his cunning blows upon it.

To the Sampo the world converges.
From the Sampo
an energy emerges
whose radiolarian saprophytes
nourish the earth they suture.

How pleased. Oh how pleased the gap-toothed
  hag
of the North. Who deftly hefts
the massive Sampo. Quickly hiding it away. In the
  arcanum
of the Copper Mountain. Nine locking charms
  she chants. To keep it safe.
Nine fathoms deep she quests. Into the
  mountain's heart.
Where the Sampo's reef-like salamandrine roots
begin their tapping.

The first one: rooting deep in Mother Earth.
Another one: alongside rolling water.
And a third one: cored into the home-hill.

And afterwards, Ilmarinen. To the virgin,
    pointing.
"The Sampo. It's done.
See: its intricate interlocking lid.
Marry me."

And the virgin. Saying, "Who. Who if I leave here
next summer or the summer after or three
    summers after that,
who will listen for the cuckoo calling
who will hear the mating warblers trilling in the
    open uplands
who will flock the doves together with awaiting
    wishes
who will gather all the cloudberries from their
    thorny thickets
who will attend to the talents of the joybirds
    moving extravagantly through the woods
to the Copper Mountain's summit
to the edges of these uplands.
I'm not done here.

Not done picking berries.

Not done singing along the lakeshores.

Not done finding new meadows.

Not done with summertime."

Ilmarinen. Dejected. Immense ursus of his form.
    His look downcast.

Wishing for home. Away from dreary Sariola.

Darkness homestead. Witch infested. Too long
    drawn in summer's

arctic sun. And the gap-toothed hag of the North
    Country. "Smith!

Are you sad?" Feeding him. Summer beer. Flat
    rye bread. Warm from the oven. Spread with
    egg butter.

The boat she suddenly conjures.

Solid wood. Copper paddle.

Gently lapping Bothnian waters. Rill patterns.
    From the wind she's summoned.

Thrumming the surface.
Then setting him moving.

Blue sea. Cloudless glass of sky surrounding.
A day.
Another.
And a third.
South at last. To his homestead.

Väinämöinen. Rune lord. Wizard singer. Waiting.
"Ilmarinen! Brother. Smith. Tell me. Is it done?
Did you forage in the forest?
Did you forge anew the Sampo?
Tell me."

And Ilmarinen. Moving to his smithy. Not
    looking up.
Making ready. A new fire.
But seeing in his mind's eye. The Sampo. Secretly
    enthroned.

In the core of the Copper Mountain.

Converging to it—the world.

Emerging from it—an undiminishing energy.

Nourishing the earth it sutures with its enormous
roots.

Intricate interlocking lid.

Image of the starry sphere.

Mirror of underworld channels.

Agarical jewels.

"Yes. My twilight machine. Yes.
I made it. I forged it. Anew."

II. PIKE AND HARP

—

I. WHERE DOES THE MUSIC COME FROM?

Here's where: from a birch tree
tap a balm. For fastening together wood, stories,
    wind.
The North Country's nuptial sun. Shining on
    Ilmarinen. Epic smith.
And the maid of Pohjola. Daughter of Louhi.
    Daughter of the North.
Their wedding. Väinämöinen. Shaman lord.
    Wizard singer. Whom the maid of Pohjola
did not choose to wed. His good will, nevertheless,
for his friend's good fortune. Their mid-summer
    blessings—
Ilmarinen and his bride. The total sun
of their days.

But she's been slain. Only weeks after. By
    Kullervo. Ilmarinen's servant.
Whom she taunted in the fields. (Kullervo himself
    would die as well. At his own hand.
For seducing his lost sister. In shame.)

The smithy's agonized aura of silence. His
    dolorous hammer.
Ilmarinen. Widowhood and loneliness. Dream of a
new companion. Spark in the smithy, blown in the
    bellows.
Gold and silver he melts there. To forge her. Like
    the Sampo. Like the sky.
First a sheep. And then a colt. At last from the
    flames—a beautiful maiden.
Head of silver. Hair of gold. Body exquisitely
    formed.
Delicate hammering renders her features—mouth,
    lashes, earlobes
smiling to softness. His wife's perfect double. But

she's motionless. Speechless. Deaf.

Cold at her core. With a mineral, hibernal frost.
Exuded into the air.

No fur, no blanket can warm Ilmarinen, epic
smith, lying there beside her.

Even Väinämöinen refusing when Ilmarinen
offers her to him.

Saying, "The splendor of gold. Gives no warmth.
And cold is silver. For all its sheen."

II. WHERE DOES THE MUSIC COME FROM?

The Sampo. Source of all abundance.

Väinämöinen shaman lord. To Ilmarinen. "To
Pohjola—dreary Sariola,

home of gloom. We'll go. To steal the Sampo.
To bring it back. To Suomi."

The Sampo. Fixed in the living earth. Under the
Copper Mountain.

By nine locks fastened to the core of rock. Three
great roots

binding it nine fathoms deep.

In the earth.

Through the waters beneath.

In the home-hill.

Even so. Ilmarinen—forger of the sky. And the
Sampo, too. He agrees to go. He wants it back.

A sword he forges first. For Väinämöinen. Iron,
steel,

gold, silver, charcoal. His slaves at the bellows.

Iron like soup.

Steel like bread.

Silver like a lake.

Gold like the tips of waves, kicked up by a breeze.

Charcoal like a cradle of earth. Earth of the
living.

In the flames. A sword. Forming.

Fashioning it finely as it emerges from the hellish
hoar-flame of the great furnace.

The work he renders. Its fineness.

Väinämöinen. Does this sword suit its bearer?

It does. Its point, a lunar incision.

Its edge, a solar scalpel.

Its haft, an astral balance.

Its tip, a horse at gallop.

Its grip, a feline poise.

Its sheath, a dog's leash.

Whirling it like a whipcord. Rapid diagram of
motion.

His quickly outflung sword arm. A scything action.

Cleaving the iron mountain. Lopping off its crown.

Immense wreckage of this unmountaining.

Epochal debris.

Does this sword suit its bearer? *Yes. It does.*

And so, their departure. On a fabulous magical
ship. The intricate network of lakes.

Working them northward. Ilmarinen at the oars.

Lemminkainen. Rash and resourceful warrior.
Also called Kaukomieli. Son of Lempi. Living
in poverty.
Abject. Sad. Who sees from the promontory the
coming ship.
His wretched village behind him. Lemminkainen.
Seeing Väinämöinen. Seeing Ilmarinen. Hearing
their plan.
"Take me. I need to leave." Then joining them.

Singing joyful songs. Väinämöinen. Girls. Hearing
him sing.
With wonder. Unexpected acceleration of the
waters. Rapids they plunge through.
Unstable ship.
Their immediate, obvious danger.

Waves churning foam. Water shifting tensely.
Rocks with excessive serrations
thrusting up. *The Song of the Waterfalls*. A charm
Väinämöinen chants.

Clash of oar in oarlock. Ilmarinen and
    Lemminkainen levering water.
Cords in their forearms—muscles' limits oarstrokes
    commit. Väinämöinen's pitching balance.
    Archaic charm
on his lips. Rune at the ready. Unhurt. They pass
    through.
Despite the danger.
Until beyond the rapids it stops. Their ship. Stuck.
    And no force
of the rowers can move them on.

What hindrance could this be? They're all looking
    for it. *There*. The pike. Lurid. Immense.
Its massive back the ship's crease had caught on.
    Hauki. World pike.
Gorged like a colossal eel. White writhe of its
    scales. Snapping jaw. Giant shoulders.
Like an albino leviathan. Obviously ancient. Kill it.
    They must! One after another trying. And
    failing.

Lemminkainen, Ilmarinen: their swords clashed
to pieces on the hide of the pike.
But Väinämöinen's solar scalpel, its hafted astral
balance. His sword.
Up he whirls it. Swift gyrating guillotine he
unleashes. Flashing through the lake's
ermine-churned waters.
And through the pike's shoulders. Snapping the
water dog's spine.
Exploding him like a burst intestine. Tail sinking
to the bottom of the lake.
Head hoisted onto the deck of the ship. Its jeweled
gore. There.

The ship—a shudder. Drifting lightly to shore.
The pike's head carved. Its parts in seven massive
kettles braised.
Minced for breakfast. Stewed for supper. By the
maidens on board the ship.
The blades of the bones they stew. Tossed on reefs
and rocks.

Väinämöinen. Rune lord. Augur in those bones he
    sees. Their cooked
pellucidity. A harp he would make from them.
From the jawbones of the great pike—its frame.
From the teeth of the greak pike—its tuning pegs.
From the hairs of Hiisi's gelding—its harp strings.
Kantele. The first dulcimer. Boys. Girls. Maidens
    and women. Warriors and half-grown lads.
All try it. None can play it.
Nor Lemminkainen. Nor the soul-sick folk of
    dreary Sariola, land of always dawning gloom.
None. Strings entangled. Teeth-pegs cramped.
    Horsehair whining.

Discord! Clenched jaws at jarring sounds.
Until at last in the lap of Väinämöinen, rune lord,
    this holy harp
is lain.

Song.

Silver shining, primeval song.

Pike bones. Fishtail plectrum. Emanating song.

Lynxes. Ermines. Squirrels. Wolves from long
journeys. Bears, their pelts

rubbed with heather they'd rolled through. In the
fir trees, eagles, nightingales, swans from snow
marshes,

deep-diving eider, hawks and finches, in the birch
trees, their

papering barks peeled to make sheets studded
with music—and older trees with lacustrine
waxy leaves—: All.

Bending and leaning. To listen to the rune
master.

Even the Daughters of Creation.

Sitting on arches of air.

Even the cloud lords. Massing on the borders.

Even the grass-bearded king of all the waves
mounted on the moving waters.

Listening to Väinämöinen's song.

Tears he weeps. Rune lord. Wizard singer. Rolling
from his cheeks.
Larger than cranberries.
More delicate than new peas.
More shapely than grouses' eggs.
Larger than a swallow's head.
Copious tears. For song. For its unheard origins.
Soaking his overcoat. Gathered at his feet. Then
pooling there.
To flow down to the edge of the blue lake. Its
surface of waters ceaselessly
sparkling. To pour beneath. To the unctuous ooze.
At the bottom of the lake.
"Who." Väinämöinen, saying. "Who can fetch my
tears. To put them in a jar.
What boy. What girl. I'll fangle you with feathers."
None. No crow. No raven. But a blue duck.
Strange blue duck. With a suctioning bill.
Diving down. To the nitred unctuous ooze. Where
the pools of

Väinämöinen's tears had already cohered.
  Transformed.
Nacred pearls of the blue mussel.
Fit for kings.
Fit for pleasure.
Jewels of song.

III. STEALING THE SAMPO

—

VÄINÄMÖINEN, WIZARD SINGER and rune lord.
Ilmarinen, primeval smith and Sampo forger.
Lemminkainen, reckless adventurer. Son of Lempi.
Oars and sails. Skimming the waves'
billowing textures. The lake's broad surface. Its
  rich protean blues.
Northward. To Pohjola. Dismal darkness
  homestead. Dreary Sariola.
The land where men are eaten.
Where women drown the heroes.

Oaring northward. Ilmarinen. Raw core of his
  strength.
Lemminkainen. Bursts of his younger energies.

Ancient Väinämöinen. Sitting in the stern.
   Trembling thunder-rudder he holds.
Gusts of foam the bow cuts through.
Northward. Through the turbid brash-tossing
   waters. To havenless Pohjola.
Terminus. The Sampo's mysterious source.

Copper-edged quayside they row toward.
Muscles worn from the long voyage.
Evening silence they step into. Quiet house ahead.
   Louhi's homestead.
Louhi. Gap-toothed hag of the North.
Squawking crane. Väinämöinen padding softly.
   His stealth the others mimic.
Groans of the porch under their shifting weight.
And the huge door. Its brittle hinges.
Beer he oils them with.
Resourceful rune lord.
Remains they quickly quaff. Remnant foam on
   their whiskers.

Sudden flare of matchlight. Soft witch glow of the
   lamplight.
Louhi. Clearing her throat.
"Heroes. What news?"
Her household. Awakening. To the early gloom.

Väinämöinen. "The Sampo. Its intricately
   interlocking lid.
Its image of the starry sphere.
Men and women. Speaking of nothing other.
We've come to behold it.
We've come to share it."

Louhi. Gap-toothed hag of Sariola. "If two can't
   portion a grouse
or three divide a squirrel,
no way can people share the Sampo. Listen!
Do you hear? *That's* the Sampo. It grinds away.
   Under the Copper Mountain.

Locked. Bound. To the underworld channels.
Rejoice!
I'm the Sampo's mistress."

And Väinämöinen, lord of song. "If you won't share
the Sampo,
then we'll take it from you."

Louhi, crone of Pohjola. Dreariest shadow-locked
Sariola.
Engorged. With rage. Arising. A gross specter.
Hideous.
Summoning even deeper anger. Calling all her
youthful swordsmen.
Drawing their weapons. Crossbows aimed. At
Väinämöinen's head.

Who unslings his kantele. Sitting quickly down.
Crossing his legs. Dressed in gray felt.

His hair and beard like fuming smoke. From
burning fresh pine boughs.
Tapping his dulcimer's horsehair strings. Gently.
Lullingly at first.
And then with defter touches. What tunes! Like
the breathing
valves of an animal.
Like an unknown necessity.
Men obeying a wish to pause.
Women bursting out laughing.
Heroes weeping.
Boys kneeling in wonder.

At last. They're still. All of them. Deep in
slumber. Lulled there.
Väinämöinen. Primeval crafty minstrel. From his
pocket, drawing forth:
Sleep needles. And fine thread. To lash all their
lids. Slowly

sewing them shut. Cinching the sutures tight.
    Like a surgeon stitching open wounds.
Or a cook threading herbs into a salmon for
    roasting.
One by one. All the warriors in the village. And
    all the people too.
Locked in lasting sleep.

Then flashing down to fetch the Sampo. To see
its intricately interlocking lid.
Its image of the starry sphere.
Its mirror of the underworld channels.
Down within the Copper Mountain.
Infixed there by Louhi's nine hexes.
Kept safe by ten strong bars of iron.

Then Väinämöinen. His aged nimble fingers with
    knuckles like flexing hinges.
Running them along the strings of his kantele.
    His Baltic

psaltery. Gently singing. At first. A clean melody.
Interfered with subtle discord. More commanding

singing. A subtle persuasive droning.
Tremors of musical disruption the Copper

Mountain absorbs. And the Sampo.
Enthroned at its core. Feeling the tune. Like a

rising up.
And a drawing down.
And now, Louhi's bars of iron. Trembling.

Vibrating to the tune.
All the securities loosening in the music.
Magic's lubrications.

Ilmarinen. Lemminkainen. Also known as

Kaukomieli. The rest of the heroes
they brought along.
Their pouches of clarified butter. Crystal-white as

beeswax.
Smearing the butter on the bars and hinges. Beer
they lather on locks and doorknobs.

And then Väinämöinen. Lifting bolts from hinges
   noiselessly.
Deftly opening the inner chamber's doors.
   Burgling silence spooking for the moment
   over them.

Väinämöinen. To Lemminkainen. "You. Son of
   Lempi. Most illustrious.
Seize the Sampo. Its intricate
interlocking lid."

Lemminkainen. Proud son of Kaleva's domain.
Hero son of Ukko. Boasting, "The Sampo!
I could move it with my toe!" Lemminkainen.
   Putting
his queer shoulder to it. Then,
on his knees. Digging his feet into the mountain's
   earth. Long slippery tractionless trenches.
Getting nowhere.
The Sampo unbudged.

Its intricate interlocking lid. Fixed. Unopened.

Its image of the starry sphere. Static but dynamic.

Throbbing with potential life.

Its roots in the mountain channels. Nine fathoms
deep.

Cool silent gloom in the underworld.

But above them, grazing on Pohjola's treeless
tundra—a colossal bull.

Fattened. But lithe. Sinewed. His horns a fathom
from tip to tip.

His muzzle thick as half a fathom.

From the northland meadows.

They lead him.

To the Copper Mountain. Into the dark
underworld chambers.

Whose massive roots of living rock they urge the
bull to plow.

To unearth the Sampo.

To unleash it from its long-threaded channels.

What brash action! The bull's heroic braying. Its
    taurean enormous intensities.
And the tremoring lid of the Sampo. The ancient
    magic locking it
to the underearth. Its incremental loosening
from its magically fixed sockets.

Väinämöinen, then. And Ilmarinen, primeval
    smith. And Lemminkainen. Lively comic son
    of Lempi.
Carrying the Sampo. From within the Copper
    Mountain.
To the boat. The Sampo's long clotted roots.
    Dangling behind them.
Like a sorceress's wicked nest of hair. Hefting it
    on board.
Its unwieldy size, unbalanced shiftings. Below the
    decks. Stowing the Sampo.
Its intricately interlocking lid. Slotted together.
Its image of the starry sphere. Unmoving.
    Absorbing shadows underdeck.

All of the thieves, then. Readying themselves. As
quickly and as quietly as they can. Launching
the ship.

The waves.
Slapping at the hull.
On the move.
The feeling of release.
The great rude morning sun.

Ilmarinen. "Have you thought of where we'll take
the Sampo?
This Sariola is witch infested. Evil."
Väinämöinen. "There. We'll take it there."
Pointing. Beyond the glowing dawn.
"This Sampo. With its sacronymic amanite lid.
To the Misty Island.
To its headland. And then we'll steal our way to
the island's end.
Where the bizarre islanders never eat.
And never fight.

There we'll keep it. Safely forever.
Its roots seeking out new nourishing channels.
In a grove of sacred birch trees."

Steering then through the waters. In the
    lengthening sunlight. Väinämöinen.
The feeling of health.
Of new life. In the water's billows.
In the sunlight's motions. Chaining and
    unchaining flashing shapes. On the water's
    surface.
Ilmarinen. Lemminkainen. Working the oars.
Great vast openness they pull sleekly into.

A day. Another. And a third. Long stretches of
    silence and daylight.
Lemminkainen. His mood. Open and loose but
    wanting more. "Väinämöinen! Where's
your song? Sing for us!" And Väinämöinen. His
    mood, cautious.

And watchful. "Too early. It's too early. For singing
   and rejoicing. But soon.

Soon. *When we see our doors before us.*

When we hear them creaking open."

But Lemminkainen. Wanting song. And
   undaunted.

Stepping to the stern. Taking there the highest
   perch.

And commencing to sing. At great volume. And
   without skill.

Discord! Expansive discord, sounding across the
   auditorium

of the waters. To six surrounding villages where
   the women

imagine animal slaughter. And the men the winter
   devil's laughter.

Near a seventh, a crane. Antique sky lord. Altitude
   navigator.

Standing on a narrow natural bridge. Above a still
   cluster of duckweed. Iridescent

green pocking waters. A vivid northward
   marshland.
A lordly gray crane. Standing there.
Counting the bones in its toes.
Magical actuary.
From whose stomach Siberian shamans sew their
   talismanic pouches.
Noble crane. Sky's vicegerent.
Tall as a man. Glaring sauroid eye. Flash of
   painted red. Crowning a black-striped head.
Hearing Lemminkainen's singing.
Stretching its wings in sudden terror. Lifting
   swiftly up. Flying
off. Reaching a great height. Over Pohjola.
To the Palearctic *taiga*. The crane's glaring
   terrified call. Its vivid clamor.
Its rough guttural alarm.
At top volume unceasing.
Throbbing over Louhi's sleeping warriors. Among
   the spellbound

Sariolans. Rousing them. From three days'
    enchanted sleep. Louhi. Awake.

In a panic. Thrashing at empty air. Looking for
    her bearings.

Finding them uncompassed. Scampering.

In a hyperventilated rush. To the Copper
    Mountain. To the hidden chamber.

Seeing its barriers smashed.

Seeing its locks destroyed.

Its massive doors flung open, leaning from broken
    hinges.

"The Sampo! Is it gone? Did they steal it?"

Yes.

Then Louhi, her rage shining, hexing loudly,

"Cloud Maiden! Mist Maiden! Hear me!

Väinämöinen. Shroud him in densest fog. Drape
    the lake's bright waters.

With thickest cloudhang."

And her fury mounting, thus continuing,

"But if this fails. Iku-Turso! Son of Äijö! Giant of
    the antique water hammer!
Pummel him. Crush Väinämöinen with your
    crashing sledges.
Batter his red boat to splinters.
Strand his crew of wicked heroes. In the pitching
    waters.
Drown them down in rushing rip currents.
But if that fails. Ukko! Sovereign god of highest
    places!
Thunder utterer. Tempest rudder.
Destroy proud Vaino. Felon sorcerer. In
    unrepentant sound and light. In bashing
    storm."

Ancient powers. Of water and sky. Hearing
    Louhi's earnest plea. Summoned. Answering
    her.
The Maid of Clouds expanding. The interceded
    light. Breathing upward.

From the lake. Thick
impenetrable billows. Then settling a stillness in
the air.

Väinämöinen. His fabulous ship. Its glistening
ruddy hull.
Afloat. Still. Unmoving.
Crushed in massing cloud. Vast pillows of a
soundless snare.
Dim daylight scattering through the fog.
Clouds of luminiferous moonlight crowding
night.
Three longs days and nights of this. Detained.
Waiting.

And then, Väinämöinen. "Clouds? Mists? What
fools worry about such foes?" Unsheathing
his great sword. That solar scalpel. Forged by
Ilmarinen. With meteoric art.

And in one great thrust, clearing the water.

Wide open.

Mead. Flowing on the edge of the blade.

Honey. Dripping from its tip.

Mists in an upward gush vanishing.

Clouds by new waves in pushes hurrying. Away.

Väinämöinen. "Move!" Shouting.

Thrusting out oars of the newly unstuck boat.

Chopping the waters.

Above, a sudden blue sky.

Organized panic.

A worried focus.

A sense of menace. Impending.

From the air's unseen core: a hoarse roaring. Its

volume gathering. The lake's crushed foam

thickening. In thrashing sprays.

Terror. Ilmarinen. Feeling it. Deep dread. Worse

than ever in his life. Like a boy. Drawing his felt
    cap down.
Over his eyes and ears.

Väinämöinen. Listening for the source. Looking
    toward the rush
of noise. Dislocated around them. Into a circle.
    Fluctuating around the boat.
Constricting and expanding. Erratically. Wicked
    howling throbs.
Until—there. Seeing it. Seeing Iku-Turso.
    Water-hammering son of Äijö.
Dread giant. Elemental lord. Gathering turbid
    waters into forms.
Lifting them high. Waves and
coils. Turning into enormous lacustrine hands.
Through which the waters seethe. Väinämöinen's
    boat. Scooped up. Tossed from hand to hand.
"Iku-Turso!" Väinämöinen. Commanding. "Water
    hammerer. Giant!

What roused you?
Why show yourself?"

Iku-Turso. Purposefully winding waterspouts for
   fingers. Around the ship's red hull.
Intending to crush it. Not listening to the rune
   lord. But answering nevertheless.
"To ruin you and your race.
To ruin Kaleva and the birch-tree postulants.
To crush you all to death by water.
To bear the Sampo back to northern realms of
   starlight.
To curse your memory forever after."

Väinämöinen. Undaunted. Summoning to his
   lofty peril
a tone he'd learned deep inside the earth. From
   the roots of birches.
From spruces. From bears' hibernating sighs.

Saying, "Iku-Turso. Ancient glamorous water
    giant. Nevermore.
Be gone. Take rest. Nevermore arise."
Väinämöinen's voice. Like earth's own cavernous
    oracle. Its timbre. Not to be denied.

And like sloshing water. In a great basin.
    Draining.
So does Iku-Turso vanish. And true to
    Väinämöinen's word. Nevermore to rise up.
A vanished name. A memory to be soughed on the
    winds of a rough day.

Väinämöinen. At the helm. Again. Steering the
    ship on its way. South. Plowing
the waves. To Kaleva. Its birch trees. Its striding
    elk in the glades. Glad days to be had there.
A daydream, lasting one moment. The next:
    Ukko. First god.

Air's ragged sovereign. Thrashing in magical fury.
   Shredding clouds. Scattering
tempests wildly before him.
His menacing unruly envoys.
Directions he effortlessly marshals.
Great howling forces he unleashes. At
   Väinämöinen's red-hulled ship.
Rocking in an avalanche of wind.
On the shore—pines and spruces scattering needles.
Grasses' tassles thrashed to vanishing.
Everywhere water's turbid churning. Ancient ooze
   rising to the surface.
A salty milk from upturned clays.
Väinämöinen. Steadfast. Eomancer. The hilt of his
   sword.
Its radiance. Its wroughtness.
The hand that holds it.
The ship's carved rudder. His other hand steadying
   it, jumping across the waves like a sneeze. Like
   a seizure.

The kantele, his precious harp beside him.

The wild lashing waves. The grim merciless
    assault. Great pounding
fists of wind.

The loose kantele. Skipping across the deck.

Ahtola. The sacred realms of water. Ahto—great
    god of the seas.

Vellamo. Goddess. These and their fluent
    attendants. Witnessing.

This vast reckless scene.

Imagining joy they had taken from Väinämöinen's
    playing.

On his harp. Made from the jawbone of the great
    water dog.

The world pike their realms had nurtured. Slain
    by Väinämöinen's solar blade.

There. Knocked loose. Like breath in the chest.
    And there, looser.

At last—tossed overboard! The kantele. Back in
the sea.
Ahtola's minions swimming it downward.
Into the water's hidden depths.

And then. Even in the thrashing storm.
Väinämöinen's tears. Visible. Streaking
his wizened face. "What I made. What I
cherished. What pleased me.
Vanished.
Nevermore.
To turn the tuning pegs of pike's teeth.
Nevermore.
To hear the tunes resonate. Through the pike
bones."
And Ilmarinen. Primeval smith. Beside himself
with fear and grief. Sobbing.
"Mercy! Have mercy on us. The saddest day."
But Väinämöinen. Regaining his composure.
Feeling fate moving him forward.

Chastising Ilmarinen. "Tears are wasted on
   misfortune. Yours and mine."
And arising. "Waters! *Restrain your children.*
   Gods! Call back your curses.
You winds! Disperse to heaven. Take off to the
   massing clouds.
Keep this vessel sound. Afloat."

And Lemminkainen. Raising prayer. "You, eagle,
   Turja's keeper.
Bring us three feathers.
You, raven, glossy with northland pitch.
Bring us two feathers.
To protect this ship. To keep its pinewood planks
   intact."

And the winds continuing to thrash.
And the foam seething wildly.
And the waves like gorging hillsides.

— : —

Crossbows by thousands. Swordsmen by hundreds.
  Louhi's warship. Groaning for war.
Oars carving waves. The warship speeding
  through the waters.
Making murderous haste. Meanwhile,
  Väinämöinen to Lemminkainen, Lempi's son.
"Climb the mast and check the skies. Tell me
what you see."

And Lemminkainen, loyal warrior, enthusiastic
  fool, saying,
"I see it clear around the sky
with one small cloud low in the north arising."
  And Väinämöinen,
feeling his age, saying, "Nonsense. That's not a
  cloud. It's a warship. Look again."
And Lemminkainen, saying,

"I see an island whose looming aspens and birch
    trees falcons and sage grouse
roost in droves in." And Väinämöinen, saying,
"Nonsense, again. It's the blood-thirsty sons of
    Louhi you're seeing. Look again. More closely."
And this time, Lemminkainen, lively now, seeing
    the northmen seethe. Over
the deck and the mast. Of Louhi's enormous
    warship.
"I see the warship of dreary Sariola.
Fitted with one hundred rowlocks.
There I see one hundred oarsmen.
And a thousand men with crossbows."

The truth of things. Rushing on him like a wild
    taunt. Väinämöinen.
"Row! You fools! Row!"

And Ilmarinen, epic smith, and Lemminkainen,
    lively sailor, gripping oars

carved from pinewood. Straining into the waves.
Their boat swaying with the work.
Its hull smooth as a seal.
Lunging forward.
Foaming cataract their oarstrokes churn. The
    wake's
fizzing clash. Hissing like high-country snow.
The stronger they row, the weaker they flee.
    Bewitched. The crone
of Pohjola gaining.

Väinämöinen, sensing doomsday, drawing power.
From the lap of earth the lake pools on.
Taking pitch. And taking tinder. Rubbing them.
    Between his fingertips.
Little resinous globule. Rolling it beneath his
    nostrils.
Then flicking it. Over his left shoulder. Saying,
    "Let a vast

and pitchy reef spread out. And a great cliff rise up.
On which the ship of the wretched hag
might shatter."

Treacherous reef. Branching outward. Ruinous
    cliff rising upward. Covering
the eastern horizon.
Its sudden, shocking appearance. The disturbing
    active magic
it portends.

Louhi's monstrous vessel. Speeding onward.
    Carving through the ceaseless churning
of the lake's waves. Then crashing.
On the black reef. The hull shredding. On the
    molars of the rocks.
Devoured in the jaws of the cliff face.
Shattered utterly. Its ribs smashed. Nothing left.
    Her archers and warriors

thrashing. In the volatile waters. "Who?"
Louhi, in agony. "Who can help me? My need
so dire."

Magic power she summons to her wrecked self.
   Breathing inland. Drawing it to her.
A sudden transforming shape expanding. A
   wicked
colossus. Five broken scythes. Six wretched
   pikes—these her talons.
Two broad curves of her tattered hull—these her
   massive wings.
Drove of murmuring starlings she bewitches.
   Like patches of glossy
fabric. These her feathers. The ship's great
   broken rudder—this her tail.
Vengeful horrid hellish eagle. Crying out. Urging
   the archers with crossbows
to climb on. Urging the thousands of warriors

to cling on. Then in a great sudden uprush—
    flying. Holding the air.
Like billows of wind in a valuable fabric. Poising.
    To attack.
Vulnerable Väinämöinen. "Who can help me?"
    Wickedly spoken. In a voice of daemonic ice.
Louhi transformed, a warbird. Repeating her
    plea. "My need. Is so dire."
Venom like saliva. Leaking acid from her jaw.

The Mother of Water, ancient goddess of lakes
    and rivers, speaking. To Väinämöinen.
"Look beneath the sunrise. She's coming."

And Väinämöinen. Turning his head, looking
    beneath the sunrise
the crone in raptorial hurry overwhelms—:
    Väinämöinen.
Seeing Louhi, a hawking warbird, perching
    already

on his masthead. The boat, nearly sinking. From
    her weight. Its portside pressing
downward. A humiliating
weight overloading it.

Dire. Dangerous unchained moment.

Jumala. Cloud lord. God on high. Ilmarinen, epic
    smith,
his fears in tatters. Pleading aloud, "Oh Creator,
    lord of the streaming sun.
Jumala. Protect us.
Like another's children.
Like the creatures of the high meadows.
Like a man who stumbles. Watch us and protect us.
And give me a shirt of flame,
a robe of fire—
let me squeeze a blaze from my fists."

Louhi. Looming there. Tensing for battle.

What swords, clashing?
What steely points, suddenly meeting?
What icicle's awl, what North Country's harrowing
    gore hanging lethally
there in her features?

Väinämöinen. Wizard lord. Sensing venom and
    feeling ancient. Speaking.
"Hail, Louhi, Pohjola's mistress, bird of war and
    witch of days!
Will you share the Sampo with us?
Halve it on the jutting headland
Waters enlume with foams the winds
wrack?"

Then Louhi. Awful eagle. Wings articulated like
a monster's colossal jawbone. Cackling.
"No. Not with you, Väinämöinen. Wretched thief.
I won't divide the Sampo. Not ever."

Downward plunging. To snatch the Sampo.
From Väinämöinen's deck.

Then Lemminkainen. Lempi's rash and loyal son.
     His sword drawn.
Its edge of iron he carves glyphs in air with. Then
     striking.
At the eagle's magic talons.
Hacking at them.
And shouting wildly, "Come down! Swordsmen of
     the North Country! Come down!
Bowmen of dreary Sariola! Hidden in these
     wretched feathers.
Come down!" Thrashing away.
At the enormous raptor.

And Louhi, crone of gloom, perched on the
     masthead. Taunting.
"Worthless Kaukomieli. Warrior fool. Liar.
     Whose mother

weeps in shame. You promised her sixty summers
without battle.
Liar! And coward."

Then Väinämöinen, sensing an otherworldly
domain of fiends. Onrushing.
The proximity to this realm—the realm of the
unliving—he intuits at that moment.
His death impending. Feeling ever more ancient.
His bane. His weird. Its pluming, feathered
aspect.
Coming steadily toward him.
Clasping then the massive worn rudder. Wearied.
But hefting it deftly upward.
And whirling it. Like an imbalanced gyrometer.
And then swinging the oaken spar
quickly down. Like a scythe through a field of rye.
Down
on the eagle's claws.
Shattering them.

All but the smallest.
A tiny talon, a little remnant
wound maker.

And then from her wings. The heroes of
    Pohjola—swordsmen and bowmen.
Splashing downward. A hundred. Then a thousand
    more.
Like Achaeans from a hollow horse.
Squadrons.
Crashing down. Cracking the ribs of the ship.
    Injuring it mortally.
Still dropping down. And scampering into action.
Like squirrels from fir trees.
Like wood grouses from birch boughs plump with
    grain.

And then Louhi. Reaching out to seize the Sampo.
    With her one remaining
little talon.

Hooking that hanging finger on its intricately
    interlocking lid.

Pausing for a second. To admire its image of the
    starry sphere.

Her deft clasp. Her surprising strength. Visible
    there in the noon glare.

And then her rapid, wresting escape. Sampo
    hooked.

Which she severs and flenses with knifing
    wing-strokes.

Hell-bent and giddy.

Its intricately interlocking lid torn to pieces.

Its image of the starry sphere now strewn in
    tatters.

The larger pieces sinking. Beneath the churned
    surface

of the great blue lake.

Drawn down into the noctual ooze at the bottom.

Implanted there, vital forms of life, despite the
    violence the crone enacted

growing then into the waters Ahto, god of the sea,
amasses ever after as wealth
to end when the moon
ceases to shine
its light of shook tinsel
down onto the earth.

The smaller pieces, puffed with air, floating there,
    on the lake's lurid surface.
And the winds tossing them shoreward.
And the waves sending them to the headland.

Billows. Wild, rocking, directed movement.
Väinämöinen. Feeling ancient. And purposeful.
    Following the floating fragments
of the Sampo. Tossed on the lake waves to the
    nearing shore.
Tumbling over the breakers. Onto the sandy
    shoreland.

Watching the pieces. Crimson fragments studded
    with pocks of white.
A small tattered veil. Splinters of that intricately
    interlocking lid.

Enearthing themselves. Purposefully. Extending
    nearly invisible tendrils into the soils of the
    headland.

Väinämöinen. Gushing with sudden pleasure.
Incanting an impromptu prayer:

"Plowing
sowing
increase
growth
shining moonlight
advancing sun—

the plains of Suomi
the lovely land of Suomi

whose life advances what death's saturations
draw from this broken Sampo."

Which Louhi, crone of witch-infested Pohjola,
curses thus:

"Whatever you grow,
whatever you plow,
whatever you sow,
whatever this broken Sampo's magic emplenishes,
I'll ruin
I'll devise endless, recurrent ruination for it—
I'll clash the moon into rocks
I'll bury the sun in the Copper Mountains
I'll hex with frost
what thou plowest and what thou sowest
and what thou so earnestly harvest.
I'll send an arctic winter noon to destroy things.
A hail of crushing iron.

A snowfall of metal filings.

Days and days of punishing cold.

I'll wake the bear. And weird her.

To destroy geldings. To slaughter the mares. To
    devour

the cattle. To scatter the cows.

I'll give you the plague. I'll slaughter you all.
    Moonlight.

As long as moonlight shines down on the earth,
    the world will forget

you ever existed."

Then Väinämöinen. Feeling weary. But feeling the
    ancient earth moving

very slowly under him. Saying,

"Spells from the North Country. Weak little
    whispers to me.

Threats from the men of the winter cataract.
    These stream around me.

The pitiless hammer of winter you pound with.

    It melts. Eventually.

God is the lord of weather.

Honey-paws of Arcturus guard the cultus of the

    northern sky. Not

you wicked northland men and women. Not your

    evil finger. With its nasty hooking claw.

Earth's grip wards what sorcery would spoil—life

in that headland approaching

an everlasting charm.

God lures maggots from Suomi corn. Spurs us to

    harvest.

So, then. Go back, Louhi. Wicked hag of Sariola.

    Mistress of gloom. Go back

to Pohjola. Forge winter's hammer.

Crush in your fists the rocks of the wicked.

Bury the dust in the heart of the mountain.

But the moonlight? Untame it.

And the sunlight? Say farewell.

And the hex of frost? Watch it lock your corn in
crystal.

An iron hail will plow your air. With merciless
furrows.

A hail of steel. Is all you'll harvest.

And the bear you weird. From the shadows of the
pines. Her jaws

lined with vicious teeth. Menacing. Preying.

On Sariola's cattle. I've seen it. Up from the
ancient earth. A vision.

Revolving around me."

And then Louhi. Depleted. All her strength.
Leaking from her.

Resuming her worn-out form. An eagle no more
but only a northern crone.

"The waves. Took my wealth. Took the Sampo."

And sighing. Hastening homeward. A tatter from
the Sampo's veil. Pinched.

By her wicked finger.

Carrying it back. To Sariola. Its only actual
wealth.

Gloom's homestead. Poor of light. Bitter
in magic.

Väinämöinen. Earth's ward. Feeling it. Earth's
ancient aura. Emanating
outward. Rushing toward the headland.
Suomi. His homeland.

Pieces of the Sampo. Gathering them from the
lakeshore.
From the margin of the sand.
The Sampo's sacronymic amanite lid. In
fragments.
Treating them as seeds. Cryptogams.
In the soil of the jutting headland. Making
furrows. With his
sword. Wrought for him by Ilmarinen.

Morning mist perfuming him. In an aerosol
of light. Shaking the seeds of the Sampo like
    spores of
dusky weather over the patterns of trenches in the
    open earth
he's made. Everywhere plumes of shook dust.

Then calling out. To the sky woven in cloud.
    A final prayer.
"Maker of weather. Maker of earth.
Let us live in Suomi
in argentious Karelia.
God's trance-hour stretched out before us
the wiles of sorcerous hags wither in.
The schemes of men unwind in.
The spells of water-sorcerers diffuse in.

Against earth envy. Protect us.
Shining midnight sun.
Beaming aestival moon.

Eastern ceaseless winds the summer rain chases:
these ward from frost, from evil brumal weather
cursed down on us from the lasting
lightless north.

A harvest and a refuge. These we'll make. From
    light
the moon draws its equinoctial silver from.
And the mesh of tendrils the Sampo draws down
into fertile shadow with
earth-gripped
oracular
enchantment."

IV. HARP OF BIRCH

—

VÄINÄMÖINEN. HIS MIND.

Moving at the pace of a driven breeze. Testing the
    branches
of the birches and oaks on the headland. *Music.*
It's time for music. But his smashed kantele—
sunk in the waters. "My joy. It's gone. To the rock
    caves
the salmon and lake pike cool in
shadows and murk
more deeply obscure.
Vellamo and Ahto.
God and goddess.
Deep water spouses. Hoarders of shadows.
And ritual magics. They'll keep my joy. Like a relic."

Another brush of mind in the branches.

    "Ilmarinen! Epic smith. Ancient forger.
Make me a rake forged of iron setting the teeth
    closely together
set on a handle of precarious length. I'll use it.
To rake the billows
to rake the waves
to comb the reeds
to groom the sedges
to find my harp
evasive pathways of fishes obscure."

Then Ilmarinen. Forging an iron rake. Fitted to
    a copper handle.
For Väinämöinen. Teeth in a length
one hundred fathoms. Five hundred fathoms
long the handle. Colossal
magical tool weirdly balanced. Wielding it
    somehow.

And setting off. To the lakeshore. Nearby. To a
   small dock. Clad in shining copper
the sunlight, interrupted by clouds in tatters,
   strobes
irregularly on. Where two boats wait.
An older and a newer one. Then saying to the
   newer,
"Go, boat that I need. Out into the moving waters."
Hopping deftly into the stern before the vessel
   speeds off guided by his magic summons.
And with his great rake, Väinämöinen, sweeping
   the waves. Combing the depths.
Grooming foam like carded wool. Gathering great
   bales of the leaves of water lilies.
Driftwood. Debris. Water rubbish. Errant feathers.
Smoothing the drifts of shoreline pebbles.
Filtering every churning current.
But finding no remnant of his great harp. Formed
   from the jawbone of the world pike

he'd beheaded. Tensely strung with daemonic
    hairs from Hiisi's mane.
Sunken dulcimer. Drowned forever.

Whisking back shoreward. Discarding his rake of
    iron and copper.
Dragging himself to a new woodland dwelling.
    Väinämöinen.
Ancient shaman lord. Feeling newly weary.
Feeling the earth
shuddering gently in its turning.
Great terminal grief dragging his footfall.
Felt cap grimed and askew. Sighing.
"Pleasure. Lost to me.
Pleasure from my harp, my jawbone harp, lost.
Pleasure from the harp I made. Gone."

And Väinämöinen wanders then
into the bright-lit woods
to cross a swollen rivulet
that marks the springtime floods.

There is no shadow he would claim.
The one across his heart
suffices to deprive him of
the workings of his art.

No music coming from his lyre.
Destroyed beneath the water.
No songs delight the northern woods
or fill the air with laughter.

Despair inspires the worst his thoughts
are capable of forming—
a loose untethered lifeless sigh
without a wizard's cunning.

Then up ahead he hears a groan.
It is a birch tree weeping.
Lamenting. Speckled branching tree.
Whose saps and resins seeping

the wizard Väinämöinen rubs
along his finger's edge.
He lifts it up; it smells of life
and takes him to the verge

of where a song might still be drawn
from nature's shining brow.
"Oh beauteous birch tree shedding tears—
Wherefore weepest thou?"

"I weep for weakness and lament
my bare-stripped trunk and place
among the willows in these woodlands
children won't deface

with knives. And yet they score *my* bark,
and draw from scars my sap,
and tear the paper girding me
to make a plate or cup.

From strips of skin the herdsmen weave
baskets with their hatchets.
They hack my limbs for walking staves.
And girls beneath my branches

cut them down to bind them up
to make their summer brooms—
and woodsmen come to clear the glen
for frolic as it warms.

When winter comes I'm stripped of life
to shiver in the frost
of bitter sunless endless days
when all the light is lost.

And so I bend here weeping tears.
Awaiting ugly fate.
And so I shiver in this wind
no windrow will abate."

Then Väinämöinen says in turn,
"Oh birch tree, weep no more.
A joyful future comes for you
because you hide the spoor

another saprophytic life
begins to mushroom from.
To you will come transfigured life
in everlasting form."

And on that glowing summer day
does Väinämöinen warp
a pleasure from the birch's trunk:
the frame of his new harp.

A core of birch he smooths to shape.
in resonant delight.
To find a sound inside the wood
he tests until it's right.

There. His harp of birch. Holding the frame of it.
  Aloft in the sifting light. Marveling at it.
Wanting to complete it. Striding quickly.
  Through the woods to the farm yard, his
  thatched wizard hut
at its fringe. Ancient oak tree spreading there. In
  its witching branches,
cuckoos. Flashing fast from bough to bough, their
  berry-red eyes. Fixed on acorns.
Their pentatonic calling—five notes sung like
  chords. Rising up through the leaves.
Floss of gold in coils winding from their bills.
  Great piles of silver tinsel too.
Väinämöinen. Seized with wonder. Collecting
  gold and silver in a five-tone trance.
Pressing the ductile precious metals with his
  thumbs. Forming knobs into pegs,
hardening magically. Tuning pegs from cuckoos'
  song.
From his wanderings, from his talismanic bag.

Väinämöinen. Arraying before him materials he
needs. To finish his task.

A blue elk's shoulder blade.

A reindeer's knee bones darkened by birch sap.

A red salmon's tail, stiff as a plectrum.

Teeth of the great pike rattling like sharp dice.

Amber hairs of a softly singing maiden he coaxed
in a valley to donate her braids.

For harp strings.

And the huge core of the birch.

On his workbench before him. Smooth hewn life
of the tree. Resonating joy.

Assembling these into his kantele. His harp. His
mystery sensorium. His forest psaltery.

Laying it on his knees. Testing the strings'
tension.

Tapping his fingers like a dulcimer's mallets.

Where does the music come from?

From a heart of birch.

From a crafting hand.

From foraged lore and forlorn loss.

From a cuckoo's golden song and a maiden's gift
of hair.

From dreary Sariola and the homestead of
Kaleva.

From a natural history of magical transformation.

From the Sampo.

From the Sampo's scattered remnants.

All you people in the villages and all you
wanderers purposefully moving.

All you boys on the ground kneeling and you girls
shedding tears.

All you men and all you women feeling pleasure.

And all you creatures untensing, your claws
unflexing.

And all you birds of the air pausing on branches.

And all you worms in the earth squeezing through
earth.

And all you sacred mushrooms unthreading your
     proteins in great silvery fungal meshes
in hectares of earth the *forestum* of pines and firs
     and holy birches spring from.
And all you cloud lords and massing forces of the
     sky and the celestium.
And all you spirits susceptible to charms
and all you transanimating daemonic powers.
Listen!
Listen up!
Väinämöinen the shaman lord, wizard of the solar
     midnight and sorcerer of the noontime moon,
is playing this song for you.

THE END

Afterword

The Sampo is drawn from the *Kalevala*, the Finish national epic, compiled by Elias Lönnrot (1802–84), a district health officer and folklorist who covered the area of northeastern Finland, known as Karelia, in his work. Gathering material and tales, Lönnrot published the first version of the *Kalevala* (whose name means something like "the abode of the Kaleva," who were an ancient, legendary people) in 1835, following with a second, final edition in 1849.

The poem involves the adventures of a cluster of heroes set in a primordial time moving through forlorn wintry landscapes and, occasionally, the midnight sun-light of summery profusion. Chief among these heroes is Väinämöinen, wizard and rune lord, old and stead-fast, and unwaveringly cunning. The poem doesn't always focus on Väinämöinen—there are also Ilmarinen, the smith, Lemminkainen, a reckless warrior, and Louhi, the sorceress of the arctic north country—but Väinämöinen's presence electrifies the verses whenever he arrives.

Väinämöinen appears as an archetypal wizard, with a long white beard, a mercurial nature, and inspiring incantatory powers. He fluently engages natural and supernatural forces alike. He pursues tasks and performs deeds of conspicuous Orphic promiscuity. Nature obeys his commanding voice. He creates the first lyre, a dulcimer-like instrument called a *kantele*. He invents song. He's reputed to be one of the models Tolkien used for Gandalf.

The Sampo itself is a deeply coveted object of mysterious power and provenance. Typically, it is described as a magic mill, grinding out salt, corn, and even coins. But that description doesn't quite suffice. Over the years, some have speculated that it is a treasure chest, or the ritual replica of an arctic world pillar that carries the sky on top of which is the Pole Star itself. The Finnish poet Paavo Haavikko even proposed that it was a fabulously wrought mint stolen by the Vikings from Byzantium, like an object out of one of Yeats's grandest poems. These all make sense, in a way, because the Sampo is clearly forged by the metallurgical arts of Ilmarinen, the blacksmith. And yet these explanations feel insufficient too, because the Sampo has obviously organic features—including great roots it extends deep into the earth—behaving at times as esoterically and as plenteously as a mushroom, a theory that R. Gordon Wasson ventures in *Soma: the Divine Mushroom of Immortality*. Whatever the Sampo is, everybody wants it.

In early July 2011, I visited Helsinki. My family and I were in Scandinavia for my wife to do research on open-air museums. We had taken a passenger ship overnight from Stockholm to Helsinki, arriving after only a few hours of darkness on a bright midsummer morning. This was something of an ancestral homecoming for me: my mother's father and all of his family were Finns who had emigrated in the late nineteenth century to the Upper Peninsula of Michigan, where, with other Finns, they worked in the mines and as day laborers. During our visit, we went to the National Museum of Finland, a great brick structure in the style of Romantic Nationalism. The entrance hall to the museum is crowned by an impressive dome, the pendentives of which are decorated by frescoes of scenes from the *Kalevala* by Akseli Gallen-Kallela, the great Finnish art nouveau painter.

Four scenes, one for each pendentive. Ilmarinen plowing a field of vipers. Väinämöinen slaying the great pike. Ilmarinen forging the Sampo. And Väinämöinen stealing the Sampo from Louhi, who has taken the form of a terrifying bird of prey. Gallen-Kallela's rendering of these scenes is heroic and highly stylized, folklorish in a sense but imbued with an elegance you could associate with the style of Gustav Klimt and Egon Schiele, masters of the Vienna Secession and whose work Gallen-Kallela's closely resembles. These are images of wild and stylish fantasy. Gazing up into these scenes, I saw my poem in a single holographic flash. I would need, of course, to write it, but I had already seen it in that instant. I bought four postcards in the gift shop, one for each fresco, and later, back home, laid them out like tiles on my writing desk, Tarot cards of an epic divination.

Later, after completing the draft of this poem, I began to think: How did this happen? How did I see the poem as a whole in a flash? Recently, I remembered a book, *Wizards and Witches*, written by Brendan Lehane and published in 1984, the first volume in Time-Life's Enchanted World series, to which my younger brother subscribed. The book's first chapter, "Singers at the World's Dawn," is devoted largely to Väinämöinen, and includes a narration of the Sampo and its theft, alongside Gallen-Kallela's *Kalevala* drawings of the wizard himself, energetic with magical battle. I pored through this series while in high school, but especially *Wizards and Witches*. So, I had already encountered Väinämöinen's story long before I saw those frescoes in the National Museum, though in the different context of fantasy and folklore, which absorbed my imagination almost completely in those years.

The Sampo is adapted from five different chapters of the *Kalevala*, each of which is called a *runo*, or rune.

"Forging the Sampo" adapts Runo X; "Pike and Harp" adapts parts of Runo XXXVII, Runo XXXIX, Runo XL, and Runo XLI; "Stealing the Sampo" adapts Runo XLII and XLIII; "Harp of Birch" adapts Runo XLIV. My versions reproduce neither the rhythm nor the meter of the original, which sounds in an incantatory trochaic tetrameter (imagine an entire epic poem in the meter of Blake's "Tyger"). Domenico Comparetti, a nineteenth-century folklorist and Homeric scholar, writing about the *Kalevala*, claimed, "In Finland ... , since there is no difference in form between *epos* and *melos*, the word rune has a wider, more extended application. The form it represents, created without doubt for magic song and then used for all other poetry, bears the mark of great antiquity."

To make my magic song, I was guided by two purposes. First, I wanted to create an imagist epic. Second, I wanted to create a poem that is a fantasy, in the sense of the popular genre—"My preferred genre," in the words of poet Tom Fisher. Toward fulfilling these purposes, I used two models. First, to a lesser extent, I was guided by the example of Christopher Logue's *War*

Music, his resetting of Homer's *Iliad* in imagist flashes. Second, and to a greater extent, I adapted a technique borrowed from the poetry of Thomas Meyer, especially his poem "Rilke," but more generally in his books *Coromandel* and *Kintsugi*. To these models, just as to the *Kalevala* itself, I have made modifications and changes to suit the purposes of my poem. But just so, my poem could not exist without these examples.

To write this poem, I relied on the text of the *Kalevala* found in the 1963 edition published by Werner Soderstrom Osakeyhtio Laakapainossaen Porvoossa, as well as F. W. Kirby's 1907 translation, Keith Bosley's 1985 translation, and occasionally, Aili Kolehmainen Johnson's 1950 prose translation, published in Hancock, Michigan, where my grandfather's family emigrated and lived beginning over a century ago. For reasons obvious and ancient, I dedicate this poem to my mother, Jan O'Leary.

Acknowledgments

"Forging the Sampo" first appeared in *Chicago Review*. "Pike and Harp" first appeared in *Reliquiae*. An initial, incomplete version of "Forging the Sampo" appeared in *From a Compos't*. Many thanks to the editors of these journals, Patrick Morrissey, Autumn Richardson and Richard Skelton, and Steven Manuel respectively.

Thanks to AIR Krems for a residency in which this poem first manifested; further thanks to the School of the Art Institute of Chicago for both the residency and a subsequent paid leave from teaching that allowed me to begin drafting the poem.

Thanks to friends and readers: Zach Barocas, Alicia Cohen, Devin Johnston, Steven Manuel, Michael O'Leary, Father Harry Potter, and John Tipton. And a tip of the hat to John Beer for his knowledge of the hierarchies of regency and how properly to express the names of their agents.

PETER O'LEARY was born in 1968 in Detroit, where he was educated by the LaSallean Christian Brothers. He studied literature and religion at the University of Chicago. He is the author of four previous books of poetry, as well as two books of literary criticism, including *Thick and Dazzling Darkness: Religious Poetry in a Secular Age*. He lives in Oak Park, Illinois, and teaches at the School of the Art Institute of Chicago and at the University of Chicago. With John Tipton, he edits Verge Books.

Published by the Cultural Society culturalsociety.org
ISBN 978-0-9887192-8-6 Designed by Quemadura
Printed in Michigan on acid-free, recycled paper